THE FIGHT JOURNAL

John W. Evans

Rattle | *Studio City, California* | 2023

Rattle Foundation
12411 Ventura Blvd
Studio City, CA 91604
www.rattle.com

CONTENTS

ACKNOWLEDGMENTS

My gratitude to the editors of *Pangyrus*, in which the poem "Lakefill" originally appeared.

My deepest thanks to the editors at *Rattle* for recognizing and publishing this chapbook. Thanks especially to Tim Green for his close editing, beautiful design, humanity, and support. I am indebted to the Creative Writing Program at Stanford University for its generous support, especially Eavan Boland and Ken Fields, as well as to the DCI Program for its generosity in our work together, especially Becca Taylor and Katherine Connor, the IntroSems Program, and the Continuing Studies Program. An emphatic second thanks to Ken Fields for being such a thoughtful reader of this manuscript. Thanks to Don Mayer, Anne Kenner, Gabriel Sama, Stephanie Wooley-Larrea, Emma LaPlante, Ben Hubbard, Bill Briggs, Patrick Noonan, Thayer Lindner, Mark Clapper, Joe Dworetzky, and Cosima Justus for reading drafts. Thanks to my first writing north stars, Ray Peterson, Mary Kinzie, and Campbell McGrath. Thanks to my family, in particular my parents, Linda and Mike Evans, for their love and support. To Walt, Sam, and Monty, my thanks and love.

THE FIGHT JOURNAL

for EB and KF

Fight

Pick up, I said, and talk to me, you said, come
home and talk to me, I said, not until we can talk, you said,
what, I said, like fucking human beings, you said, I won't talk
to you, I said, until you come home, you said, I won't call back,
I said, then don't, you said, I can't come home until
we talk, you said, who does this, I said, talk to me, I
said, no one does this, you said, someone is doing it, you said,
right now, you said, people don't, you said, act like this, I said, I'm
trying to talk to you, I said, just come home, I
said, can't we talk, you said, come home
first, I said, I left home, you said, so we can talk,
you said, no one talks, you said, not like this, I said, just
talk to me, I said, I am, I said, talking to you, you
said, what did I just say, I said, it matters how you say it,
you said, this is how I said it, I said, pick up, you said, come home.

The Fight Journal

1.
The psychiatrist listens, then says
I'm handling things about as well

as anyone in my situation could.
I'm remarkably accepting of what

is happening, she says, and that's good.
I'm "deriving a sense of self from my responsibilities"—

I write that one down for later—
and people don't always do that.

I'm working. I'm sleeping. I'm even
reorganizing the house. More than anything else,

clearly, I'm thinking about the boys.
I'm enjoying my time with my children,

and people don't always do that, either.

2.
The day my wife moved out I hired
Christopher to put together new furniture:

two bright yellow bookshelves, the weird
glass cabinet thing, the front table,

a small side table, the tall bookshelf
I bought to make a comic book library

and hold the new PlayStation. I was
trying to make the house less fancy.

I wanted to replace my wife's antique furniture
on the cheap. Really, I wanted the boys

to come home from school and see
that things were still in order

at Dad's house. I was jealous, a little
threatened even, when they saw Mom's new place

and loved it: the tiny duplex next to
the Safeway in our old neighborhood.

It had vines growing over the walls
and seeds she had already swept

to the corner of the patio, under a rusted grill.
The boys' beds were bunked.

She had painted them yellow and green.
"Well, Dad," Walt said after finding the little

courtyard where he could practice soccer,
"at least you get the bedroom all to yourself now."

3.
A week earlier, we had followed exactly
the mediator's script and, as suggested,

my wife had taken the lead. It was her decision,
the mediator said, so she should tell the boys

and explain it the way a four-year-old could understand.
Mommy no longer loves Daddy the way a wife loves a husband.

*I don't know why. Why do your shoes change size
from year to year? Why did you like soccer in the fall*

[...]

and baseball in the spring? "The kids probably know
already," the mediator said helpfully,

and later I thought it was indeed strange
that there wasn't more accountability

to the act, as though it was as easy
to stop being a family

as it was to decide, okay, time to put away
the baseball mitts and pull out the soccer cleats,

but my wife only got to "divorce" before they all
stormed out of the room, crying, and when

she felt overwhelmed, helpless, heartbroken,
she went to Target, and when she came back,

I had the boys settled and eating Indian food,
though no one really wanted to watch *The Avengers*.

4.
"Going to Target" had been code all summer
for driving around, talking to her sister on the phone,

then coming home resolved again to divorce.
This lasted about seven weeks. At first

she said she didn't have a plan, really, just the certainty
that things were over. She was done. I slept

on the floor of the office for a few days,
then we switched between office and bedroom,

a kind of competitiveness and evening
up the score that characterized

how I responded to her betrayal,
with one-upmanship, and who-could-suffer-more.

The boys came to whoever was in the bedroom.
That was odd. I hated the boys

ever sleeping in our bed, but as soon
as the divorce started I made space

for the boys and the dog. I slept right at the edge.
I pulled another mattress onto the floor

when I wanted to sleep by myself,
though I did this less and less,

especially after she moved out.
I missed the boys when they were gone,

and after a while, they slept
only in my room, and my niece

moved into the guest room, then a soccer
coach. I hated being alone.

5.
When the dog thing happened in January
the fighting got bad. It had never been good,

we agreed, but it got worse
after the dog thing. She discovered

all at once that she had been unhappy for years
and just didn't know it. She insisted

I get a psychiatric evaluation. She
said that I seemed sick. The psychiatrist said yes,

[...]

you have panic attacks. You are vigilant
and insecure. This is not uncommon for people

who survive bear attacks. For widowers.
An antidepressant might help.

I was hopeful that she would change her mind
if it was just that I was sick.

I agreed our problems were my fault
and there was nothing to be done.

In dog court the judge ruled
that the fight wasn't our fault. We didn't have

to kill our dog like the other owner had wanted.
But my wife said again: she had been unhappy

for years and she just hadn't seen it,
and now that she knew she was unhappy

how could she ever stay?
Didn't she deserve to be happy?

6.
"These are fixable problems," the first
marriage counselor explained,

"some couples just get too tightly wound."
And when the second counselor said it, too,

my wife yelled at both of us.
"You guys act like this is a wake-up call

but I'm *fucking doing this!*" She went for a hike
in the Sierras a few weeks after that

and called me, angry. "You know what really
sucks about this?" she said, crying. "Everyone will

think it's *my fault*. That I just didn't try hard enough."
"You didn't," I said finally, "you're not trying at all,"

which still feels like the truth,
though it did nothing to win her back.

7.
What I thought at first was this: she ran for the hills.
She saw a lousy therapist.

She didn't want to be anyone's wife.
What the mediator said was right: she didn't love me

and on some level, probably, we didn't love each other
enough at least to stick it out, to make amends

rather than just to forgive and forget,
which didn't happen so often either. "Disclosure

is over-rated," the second counselor said at our follow-up visit.
"Plenty of people have it worse or better."

What did it matter that there had been good times?
The good times had not lasted

long enough to make her miss them,
while the best memories—

the kitchen dances, the parties, the trips,
the long afternoons sitting on the grass

at her parents' house, reading
and talking about the kids—

[…]

were changed, too. It was like they had
happened to neighbors we heard fighting late at night.

"Togetherness ruins American marriages,"
my Irish boss said one afternoon, sitting

on a bench by our office. "My husband and I
refuse to do anything together. We have for years."

8.
Divorce changed how I thought about my first marriage,
too. I missed Katie

without complication. In a dream we talked
for the first time since she had died. She told me

it was all fine. She wasn't mad at me
for remarrying. Nothing was meant to last forever.

She was wearing a blue windbreaker
and we were sitting beside a lake

watching my second wife's family walk up a hill.
It didn't occur to me until a few hours

after waking that this was where she had died.
I got mad at myself, my brain, my heart

for coopting the place as consolation.
"You can't control a dream," the psychiatrist said,

but I was pretty sure I could. I had
dreamt of Katie, what, two or three times, since she died?

When she went to college
Katie received her Catholic confirmation.

I started going to church after my second wife left
and praying the rosary daily,

a kind of transactional deal, probably,
that I wanted to strike with God,

though the comforts of prayer continued
long after the divorce was finalized.

That first week I turned off my phone
and sat at the confessional grate.

It was a Saturday, miserable and hot.
No one else was in the church.

"We get a lot of widows," the priest said.
It was the same thing the tattoo artist had said

when I got the memorial tattoo for Katie.
A different tattoo artist that week burnt

a line from Paul's epistle
advising the Thessalonians to wait,

to give thanks for the good news, and burden
no one with sins or charity—

advice I have never followed in my life—
onto my chest, then took a photo for his book,

and a few months after that
he carved next to it a tree my niece

had sketched on a piece of wrapping paper
to celebrate our first Christmas together since Katie's death.

9.

It's true. I was incredibly pushy and clingy. I had to talk
about everything, all the time. Sometimes,

most of the time, I had no idea
who I was unless I was her husband,

a father, a real family man who tells stories
and watches excellent television shows with his wife

after the kids go to bed. It was all a package.
She hated her part. She wanted the divorce

to be done before the school year began.
And she got mad, really mad

that I hadn't acted cruelly, I
think, because she had wanted to have a big fight

right away, at the start of summer, so that everyone
would see how hard it was for her,

so that she would have no choice but to leave.
She had packed a bag in the car

on the advice of a lawyer or friend, who said
you never know how men are going to act

when they feel threatened. Better safe than sorry.
Most of her friends knew about the divorce before I did.

She said she had decided it all at once,
it had come like a revelation:

I don't have to put up with this shit anymore.
Which meant, I realized much later, that

however we talked, most every night, about what
could be changed and what couldn't, however she felt

like she was drowning in quicksand and had
gotten to the edge of the pit, so that she could breath

free if she only got away, this was her one
chance to get away—if she didn't

do it now she would never *live her one true
life*. Her words, not mine. She

had wanted to do yoga in Costa Rica
and travel with friends to Palm Springs.

I said, then do it. Today. This week.
She said I was missing the point.

I only understood much later was what she meant:
with me none of it would happen. She would never be happy.

She had worked this all out at once
and during all of the years we were married.

10.
She said several times, when she was really angry,
"Of course *you* don't want to get divorced.

You've got a great deal!" I agreed that I did.
She said this a lot after she asked for a divorce.

She saw my desire to stay married as the ultimate weakness
of vision. We were unhappy. Things should not go on.

"In sickness or in health," I said, confused,
but also, bitter. She hated that, too. I had

[...]

a tremendous capacity for saying unfair things,
which to her, meant, I think, no accountability,

a terrific attention to contracts
long expired. "I wasn't born with your Catholic

shit," she said. "I don't feel guilty. Relieved,
maybe. Sad. But I refuse to feel guilt."

11.
She had kept a fight journal for three years,
she said, to vent her anger after fights.

It became gradually a record of grievances
about my meanness and pettiness,

the menacing bears and looming mountains,
my waking nightmares and insecurities,

the boys and all that boy energy in the house
when what she wanted was a daughter

like her mother who had three daughters
and did not believe in therapy. Alcoholism, either.

"I know her father from meetings," a friend said.
"He's always just about to quit drinking,

it's thirty years now." I learned to ignore that,
too. We ignored everything until we didn't.

"You're a noisy bottom," a friend said.
"You'll take it, but you complain like hell."

"Okay," a different friend said, "but where's
her happiness journal?" It felt like playing

ping pong on both sides of the net
with no one keeping score.

It wasn't the happiness she tracked or that felt
like enough. It was happiness

she wanted to forget because it felt
like a trick I played

to keep her from leaving,
offering everything. She was certain it wouldn't last.

12.
"Who the fuck keeps a fight journal?"
my lawyer said the first time we talked,

shaking her head. "I've never
heard that one before."

13.
When Monty was sitting in her lap
after we told the boys, crying hysterically,

I said to my wife, "Tell him about your *happiness*!"
When Walt had to miss school that week, I asked her,

"Did you tell him about your *happiness*?"
"I'm losing the divorce weight!" I declared

one evening getting out the shower,
and she scowled. "Too soon?" Even hurt,

I was still pretty funny but the humor,
as always, was mean. I wasn't helping anything.

[...]

14.
After the dog fight I couldn't get out of the car.
I just sat in the driveway, thinking about bears

that night on the mountain, wondering who
was coming to save Katie from hers, and when my wife

called my old friend, Bill, it was Bill and not my wife
who talked me out of the car. I sat in the chair

by the door most of the night. The next morning
I called my doctor. That was what troubled her.

"I've seen you in crisis," she said, shaking her head,
"and this just isn't it." But it was, at least

the psychiatrist said so after the work-up,
and that made her want to leave even more.

We had used up together all the hope,
and there was nothing to say about what lingered

still between grief and injury,
where all the feelings came out

again and again, and we could make no sense
with words of what we felt

except that what felt still to me like love
felt to her, more and more, like a secret she kept

to herself, one she harbored no illusion
of ever explaining to me.

She was done with trauma.
She had lost any hope that either of us was well.

15.
The week before she left I made a list
of twenty-eight things I had either done

or was willing to do to save the marriage.
I gave it to her in a letter. I said

I would do anything, change anything. She could do
anything. I didn't want the old way of marriage either.

"It's like you guys are fighting a PR war,"
a friend said, "in a newspaper that no one is reading."

He wasn't wrong. We lost the thread of every story.
We retreated into our respective camps

of friends and family who, at best,
wished us well but wanted no part of the drama

except to agree that we each were right,
which was all that we asked. What else was there

to control except the opinions of those
who would always choose to love us?

They sided with us. Mine agreed it was all
a tragedy. Hers wished me good riddance.

Before she left she gave me a list
of everything I had done wrong:

five pages, typed and single spaced,
full of typos and bullet points,

hardly a list at the end,
and full of exclamation points.

[…]

16.
"It's someone else," my sister-in-law kept saying.
"No one gets divorced this fast unless there's someone else."

17.
Here's what I think. I think my wife quit.
I think she walked out on the boys and me.

I think she would rather feel confused or helpless
or angry than hurt. I think a person reaches a certain

age and just decides to either want a life
or not to want it. Or do the work. Fuck the vows.

My wife hated work. It reminded her of things
that did not happen easily. We had married easily,

me a couple of years after I was widowed,
her as soon as I arrived in San Francisco.

It worked like that, at first, so easily,
nearly an exchange: we played house together,

I no longer had to think seriously about life and death,
she did not have to wonder about being alone.

We wrote our names on everything
and made a life together: pure genius

how the heart and hurt mended each other
in our separate bodies, how we mistook

the absence of conflict
for proof we would never hurt each other,

a foolish, consistent polish on our little minds,
like fresh paint on rust keeping bright

the places we saw our reflections in each other,
and ignored the growing hollowness,

a corrupt notion of salvation,
that we either deserved it or we didn't.

We were elect until we were not.
Even my company made her feel wary and suspect.

18.
"Congratulations, Dad," Walt said when I followed
him upstairs that afternoon, his eyes red, shaking his head but no

longer crying. "Now you can get married a *third* time."
He was eight years old, our oldest, a sweet boy,

dramatic like his father and eager to sting when hurt.
"This isn't how you *do* it," he said to both of us.

"You're supposed to show us movies for months
that have people getting divorced at the end.

Then you read us books. *Then* you tell us."
Later: "You have to get that *LOVE* tattoo removed

because Mom doesn't *love* you anymore."

19.
I got the *LOVE* tattoo in March as a reminder of the year
I had lived with Katie's family after her death.

My niece, who had moved to Oakland, sat up with me
watching *Fleabag* and talking about that year

she had known me as her live-in uncle, and all the fun
we had had since she moved to the Bay Area.

[...]

I had intended to get a full sleeve that my wife
and I had sketched on a diner napkin after a fight:

little totems of my life ringing the arm, Kansas City
to Chicago to Bangladesh to Miami to Romania

to Indiana to California. Things were good that March.
At least I thought things were good enough in March

to end the totems at my wrist, where the cuff
of a dress shirt would hide the ink.

That's how I thought about privacy then:
it hid away what you didn't want others to know,

and if they didn't know it, then surely
I was still the person they saw, the good man

who could trick others into believing
he was someone he was not,

a definition of "shame" that I read in a self-help book
when I no longer believed the answer

to saving our marriage would come from us,
when I still could not accept that our marriage was unsavable,

and I looked everywhere for help. I was naïve,
unflappable. Every problem had a solution.

It did not occur to me yet that, to her, I was the variable
she had worked, again and again, for years

hoping to find the solution.
She had her answer.

I got the *LOVE* tattoo on a Wednesday
on my forearm, near the elbow: Robert Indiana's

holiday greeting of words and signs.
"It will look great," my wife said, "whatever you get,"

a plausible deniability, that, just as when
she called Bill after the dog thing she offered no rationale:

"John will need an advocate now.
He needs someone to take care of him."

20.
The dog thing was awful. It went on
for months. Cops and lawyers. A deposition

from a trainer who refused to find fault
sealed the deal. Our dog was happy.

He was not a dog's dog. Well,
who was? It costs eight thousand dollars

to hire a canine advocate. My wife and I
walked all the way out to the Bay,

arguing that one back and forth.
In the end, she went alone because

the judge, we were told, would be more sympathetic.
He issued a ruling right away

but it got lost in the mail. Six weeks
later, we were acquitted. By then,

my wife was texting her therapist every day.
"Didn't I tell you I was seeing a therapist?"

she asked at our celebratory dinner.

[…]

21.
I believe this, too. My wife and I got together
from a great distance we both romanticized,

me the wounded and wise young widower
heading West, she the caring friend who welcomed

me to the promised land of California,
into her family, to make things better.

For the longest time, it was indeed romantic.
The marriage worked. We dated a week before

we talked engagement. We married
less than a year after that. I proposed to her

on a bridge in Chicago,
at the end of a long scavenger hunt

guided by family and friends. She said yes
right away. She refused to let me get down

on one knee. We were married six months later
and she was pregnant four months after that,

and again nineteen months later, and twenty-three
months later again our third son was born,

and she packed all of the kid stuff into boxes
and sent them to her sister in Oregon,

explaining we could buy it all again
if we wanted a fourth,

and I think that was a sign, too:
we had always planned to have four children

but she decided on her own
that three was plenty.

22.
What followed was the other side of romance:
a remoteness from everyday life, a fidelity

to fantasy even when it exceeded the reality
of a life with three kids under the age of eight.

Couldn't we still work it out?
Had we really come to the end?

I missed my wife. I missed having
a wife. "You really screwed it up,"

her sister said when I called to ask for help.
"We've been waiting for years to pop the champagne

and get our girl back,
as soon as she signs the divorce papers."

Her family was mad about that, too:
why couldn't I just face

facts that the marriage was over
and leave them alone already?

23.
"That sounds like the work of the devil,"
the priest said when I told him about the phone call.

I felt ashamed for sharing that, tipping
the scales in my favor. So I told him everything

[…]

I had done wrong in the marriage.
This took an hour. Finally, he interrupted me.

"You're being awfully selfish,"
he said. "You both are."

24.
I told him also how, the night a bear
broke into the cabin, she came tumbling down

the loft ladder, air horn in hand,
and scared away the bear. I was sleeping by the door

because I had been sick all night,
going to the outhouse and back,

something in the water, some bad food
I had picked up on my drive to the mountains.

All summer, our youngest imitated the pitch
of the air horn, running into different rooms in the cabin,

screaming, laughing and then running back out.
He was not afraid of bears,

which seemed like a kind of victory,
a break in the pattern,

which is what I suppose scared her the most:
that anything could change happiness

into sadness, a place of refuge into terror.
That, for the rest of her life, unpleasantness

would tincture what she loved
or mint love with hatred,

passing in the world currencies
indistinguishable even by their sum.

I had felt this way about love since the beginning,
that love and hatred could happily coexist,

but she could hardly tell them apart.
"Acceptance," the priest said, recommending a prayer,

"and try not to think about yourself so much."
So I kept praying the rosary, and felt

like a child, spending so much time alone
when the boys were with her,

and in this way I tried that most awful
cliché of contemporary life,

gratitude, which was a kind of prayer, too,
the tattoo on my chest:

"In all things give thanks,
for this is God's will for you."

25.
"Your uncle," she told my niece, "is a wonderful dad."
She shook her head. "I just can't live with his demons."

26.
"I do love your mom," I told the boys, "and no,
I don't want to get divorced." The mediator had said

to tell the boys the truth, even
if it felt like the wrong thing to do. Just don't

[...]

lie. I said to Walt as we lay together on the bed,
"She needs to do this to be happy,

and we want her to be happy. So, yeah,
I support this." The mediator's words

but with my own spin. *I don't want this
either*, which I didn't. Wasn't that the truth?

27.
"People go through all kinds of hell with divorce,"
the psychiatrist said. "They drink. They get DUIs,

the men especially. They can't get out of bed.
They lose their jobs. They run away.

They hurt themselves. I can't tell you why
your wife is divorcing you but I can tell you

that you'll get through it. You won't like it. But in time
you'll even think this was a good thing, that's just

how the brain works. And later, when the boys
are older and you are weaker, you

might feel like your whole adult life has been
a lie, rather than one decade in a marriage.

Better to get it all done now,"
she said. "Just rip the band-aid off."

28.
My wife stuck a series of drawings her brother-in-law
made of me right after the divorce

into the fight journal. In all of them
I was wearing a Cardinals cap

and begging my wife not to leave me,
or promising her that I would win her back.

A year into the divorce Walt found the journal
sitting open on her kitchen table.

When I asked her why she still kept a fight journal
she said she didn't have to answer my questions

anymore, though she did concede to the mediator
this hadn't been a wise choice

for Walt, who told me also she'd pasted photos of bears
into the journal with little captions mocking my fear of them,

a different kind of cartoon. Walt said
the drawings were wrong since I was a Royals fan

and bears can't talk. Later,
when our youngest broke down in tears

at his grandmother's house, and asked why his parents
had to get divorced, she told him,

"Your mommy is a nice person who does not like to fight."
"Yes," the mediator said, laughing. "That is a cheap shot.

But you're still both caught in the same thing: blame.
Who cares why the divorce happened? It happened.

Why do plagues happen? Or natural
disasters? Why do the people we love die?

Who cares what grandma thinks? She's entitled
to her opinions. Believe me, your boys

[…]

are going to have their own opinions soon enough,
and you're probably not going to agree with those, either."

29.
Eleven years ago we married.
Soon, it will be twelve, fifteen, fifty.

It was always a kind of time I marked
in error, as achievement. I dated

a woman after that and then another woman.
The time came when I did not think

at all that I had lost something
or that something continued in my heart

beyond my boys, that gift
no other life could have brought me

anywhere else, which would not be this life
in which I grieved the loss, and grieved again.

I felt this way after my first wife died:
eager for consolation, and perhaps

my second marriage was the consolation
I sought in excess of what I had lost the first time,

a consolation that ended without grief,
an ex-wife alive in the world

who would not compete for my affections,
who wanted our marriage to end when it did.

I prayed to let that go, too, or tried to let go,
a boy in the small, playful body of a man,

three boys in fact, already
becoming men, who would learn

to love, too, with imperfection
but clear of any buoyant sense

the world owed them something else,
or owed it to them for all of a life.

30.
Bill called right after the divorce. "Your first book,"
he said, "was *Young Widower*. The second

was *Should I Still Wish*. Maybe you should just
call the next one, *Nope*." I'm against epiphanies

but I'm still working like hell to find one. "So *that's*
why Mommy was sleeping in the guest room,"

Walt said finally, as I carried him back downstairs
from his bedroom. "Yeah, bud," I said. "That was it."

Lakefill

Summer in Chicago. Day five
with the cousins.
You are with your sister at a different lake.
When you come home we will divorce.
We have not told the boys,
who are running to the edge of Lake Michigan
and back up the hill,
playing a game of war with three sides.
They are just old enough I no longer worry they will survive.
The Lake is low in June.
I show my sons the first place I took you
to show you something about my life:
concrete slabs
that press the campus footprint
in a shape of water
winged in grass,
this place of anniversaries
where something now will not be remembered.
I know we sat together much farther down the lakefill,
near the beach.
There was a feeling of first seeing the Lake
that I wanted to describe to you,
how the ice and snow made places
firm enough to start in any direction.
One night I nearly walked to Wisconsin
with a friend.
On the bright ice
we traced the jeweled campus
and the water beneath us made no noise.
The water in the Lake does not rise this close to shore.
It only comes and goes,
trapped in places
where it keeps making the same mistakes.
Our oldest son
who looks the most like me

calls me over to a fresh-painted rock.
"Is this the place you said to spread your ashes?"
He remembers his great-grandfather's funeral
and the giant bowl of ashes in your closet.
"Yes," I say.
His brother starts crying.
What is written on the slabs
makes them beautiful:
marriage proposals, half rainbows, bits of verse
from yearbooks:
Not all those who wander are lost.
We love the things we love for what they are.
Near the path
I stop to take a photo
of these last days before the divorce:
three boys facing the water
in soccer jerseys.
Our youngest son is nearly floating across a blue sky.
His brother is jumping between the rocks,
across the water.
What is written on these stones
can be read clearly
even in winter, under the ice.

Musicians at the Wedding

All week at the wedding
the musicians keep practicing

over the garage, during the rehearsal,
in the basement at night,

on the back porch while it rains.
Even the grass after the rain

worries someone in the kitchen.
The tables and caterers, the flowers

and the muddy road to the barn
are covered in lights. This is a good time,

someone says, to take five, guys,
or fifty. The musicians are soggy, too.

They start again: five or six bars
of the bridal march, the chorus, the last encore.

On the porch a bartender is humming
the first dance as he bins the ice and juices,

orange and lemon. His cherries
are staked on tiny plastic swords

the wedding guests will make a great show
of plucking hilt-first.

They stand *en guarde*,
a warning term in fencing,

the first sport played in the Olympics.
In the original *en guarde* position fencers

held their back hand in the air
to lift lanterns during duels.

Back and forth to the bar the guests
litter the grass with broken promises.

This is what happens when you fall
in love: you dance all night, you collapse

for one reason or another
into the wet grass.

Fireline

And when I heard the two cabins might burn down
at the same time, on maybe even the same day,
I rooted for the fire. Like many Californians

I followed with great precision and attention
the interactive, up-to-the-minute digital maps
that showed a progression of devastation past the water's edge

of the popular tourist destination
where my ex-wife's family
had leased summer cabins since the 1920s,

where even that spring they had gathered to enjoy
the beautiful, pristine wilderness
of land the state said belonged to no one.

It was a technicality, that
outrageous claim renewed every ten years
by legacy, a claim I had once enjoyed

in an elaborate festival of coming together
we called a marriage: ten years,
then somehow faster and less forgiving

the controlled burn of divorce
that took it back. It only took a few months
to reach the woods and the lake.

The second cabin was half the size of the first
and much closer to the fireline.
All it had to do was catch

one spark near the composting toilet
and the surroundings cabins would tremble. Unfair,
that spark that every day kept not catching,

as fist-sized embers crowned the trees.
It was the old growth. I knew they'd fight the hardest.
I had fought against it for years, the impossibility

we might still love each other. We might reclaim together
the thing she did not want me to have. So
I imagined it myself. Every day the fire took a little more:

Great-Grandma Pummie's game trophies,
Uncle Chum's Turkish rugs, Puck's first editions,
all swept up into the pyro-cumulus and out across state line,

with every last remnant of these families and what they cherished.
But the redwood decks and lead-glass windows,
the rockfalls and surrounding acres of old-growth forest

hung in, as sturdy as my dog's chin on my knee.
He watched me watch the screen. When it was time
to walk, the sky had changed to orange, then blue.

Then, the wind shifted, capricious and weary of the granite.
The people returned. Their cabins were there.
In the city around the lake bears had broken in

and filled their bellies
with syrup and thawed steaks,
an early hibernation, a carcass every few yards

stuck in the mud with singed or infected paws.
Who is left to love what is gone
if it belongs to no one else;

who dares warm his hands over the ash
or rub his chest with the spite-tongued black,
murmuring, *Mine, still mine. You do not belong to someone else.*

ABOUT THE RATTLE CHAPBOOK SERIES

The Rattle Chapbook Series publishes and distributes a chapbook to all of *Rattle*'s print subscribers along with each quarterly issue of the magazine. Most selections are made through the annual Rattle Chapbook Prize competition (deadline: January 15th). For more information, and to order other chapbooks from the series, visit our website.